P9-DNK-451

AND ON THANKSGIVING, PEOPLE EAT TURKEYS!

THEY ALSO EAT CHICKENS AND DUCKS, AND QUAIL AND PHEASANT!

THANKSGIVING IS A BAD TIME TO BE A BIRD...

WOOF!
SCHULZ

CHARLIE BROWN'S 'CYCLOPEDIA

Super Questions and Answers and Amazing Facts

Featuring Holidays

Volume 12

Based on the Charles M. Schulz Characters

Funk & Wagnalls, Inc.

Photograph and Illustration Credits: The Bettmann Archive, Inc., 557; © Dan Budnick/Woodfin Camp & Associates, 532; Bureau of the Mint, 537 (top); Russell Burden, 533; © C. Harrison Conroy Company, 548; Anne Miller Christensen, 549; Eleanor Ehrhardt, 568; French Government Tourist Office, 560; Hawaii Visitors Bureau, ix; Charles R. Luchsinger, 543, 571; The Metropolitan Museum of Art, Mr. & Mrs. Isaac D. Fletcher Collection, Bequest of Isaac D. Fletcher, 1917, 547; The Metropolitan Museum of Art, Gift of Mrs. Loretta Hines Howard, 1964, 572; The Metropolitan Museum of Art, Gift of J. Pierpont Morgan, 1900, 563; Miller Services/Alpha Associates, Inc., 561 (inset); National Gallery of Washington, Andrew W. Mellon Collection, "George Washington" (Vaughan Sinclair portrait) by Gilbert Stuart, 537 (bottom); NFB Photothèque, photo by Kurt Kammersgaard, 561; Meara C. Nigro, 566, 567; Peter Pernice, 531; Belle Pressel, 571 (inset); Roberta Pressel, 570; Harold Roth, 553; Smithsonian Institute, National Portrait Gallery, 536 (bottom); United Press International, 529, 536 (top), 558; The White House/Mary Anne Fackelman, 551; Wide World Photos, Inc., 535.

 Published in the United States by Random House, Inc., New York, and simultaneously in Canada by Random House of Canada Limited, Toronto. Distributed by Funk & Wagnalls, Inc., New York, N.Y. Manufactured in the United States of America
ISBN: 0-394-84561-7

4 5 6 7 8 9 0

A large part of this volume was previously published in *Charlie Brown's Fourth Super Book of Questions and Answers.*

Introduction

Welcome to volume 12 of *Charlie Brown's 'Cyclopedia*! Have you ever wondered what a shofar is, or when people began sending valentines, or how April Fools' Day got started? Charlie Brown and the rest of the *Peanuts* gang are here to help you find the answers to these questions and many more about holidays. Have fun!

Holidays Around the World

Yesterday and Today

Has New Year's Day always been January 1?

No. Most countries in Europe did not make January 1 the first day of the new year until about 1600. England waited until 1752. Before those dates, the Christian countries of Europe celebrated the new year on March 1 or March 25, at the start of spring. In some parts of the world today, people celebrate the new year when the first green of spring appears.

January 1 was the first day of the new year in the Roman calendar. That calendar was very much like the one we use today. About 40 years before Jesus was born, it was put into use by Julius Caesar (SEEZ-ur). But people thought New Year's should be in March. So the idea didn't really catch on for many hundreds of years.

Times Square, New York City, on New Year's Eve

Why do some people make a lot of noise on New Year's Eve?

Thousands of years ago people believed that evil spirits roamed the earth. They thought that the spirits were especially dangerous at the new year. People made loud noises at the moment the new year began to scare away the evil spirits.

Most of us don't believe in evil spirits anymore. But we still make loud noises when the clock strikes twelve on New Year's Eve. Blowing horns and shaking rattlers and noisemakers are a lot of fun.

Why do people make New Year's resolutions?

People want the new year to be filled with happiness. So they resolve, or decide, to make some improvements in themselves starting January 1.

Resolutions go back a long way in New Year's celebrations. The month of January is named for the ancient Roman god Janus. He was the god of doorways and beginnings, and of comings and goings. Whenever Romans started anything new they made sacrifices to Janus. This means that they took flowers, fruits, or animals to a temple that honored Janus. The Romans always sacrificed to Janus at the start of the new year. They hoped the sacrifice would bring them the god's favor in the months ahead.

Resolutions can be a kind of sacrifice, a promise to give up something even if it is only a bad habit.

How do the Chinese celebrate their new year?

The Chinese New Year's Eve and New Year's Day are quiet family days. Then the celebrations get livelier. There are parades almost every day. Musicians, clowns, and dancers in the parades do funny things that make people laugh. The celebration lasts 15 days.

Americans celebrate Chinese New Year

How does the Chinese New Year celebration end?

With the Festival of Lanterns. The Chinese make beautiful lanterns from silk, papier-mâché (PAY-pur muh-SHAY), and glass. They shape some to look like cars, fish, dragons, animals, airplanes, and Chinese houses. The lanterns hang outside houses and in gardens. They hang along streets and in front of shops and temples. Some stay up during the whole 15-day celebration. People add still more for the festival.

When the sky gets dark on the festival day, the people parade with many lanterns. Boys wear fantastic costumes and prance about on stilts. The highlight of the evening is a papier-mâché dragon. It is often as long as a passenger-train car. Sometimes it takes as many as 50 men and boys to carry the dragon along.

In Burma, people celebrate the new year by throwing water on each other!

What is Rosh Hashanah?

Rosh Hashanah (ROASH-huh-SHAH-nuh) is the start of the Jewish New Year. It means "Head of the Year" in Hebrew. Rosh Hashanah is always either in September or October. Some Jews observe it for one day, but for most it is a two-day holiday. Rosh Hashanah is the beginning of the Ten Days of Repentance (rih-PENT-unts). During these days, Jewish people think about their lives. They repent, or feel sorry about their sins. They look for ways to improve themselves.

On Rosh Hashanah, Jews pray in the synagogue (SIN-uh-gog), the Jewish house of worship. After the synagogue service, they gather with their families for a festive holiday dinner.

How do Jews observe Yom Kippur?

Yom Kippur (yom KIP-ur), or the Day of Atonement, is the most sacred day of the Jewish year. It is the day on which Jews atone, or make amends with God, for their sins of the year just past. It marks the end of the Ten Days of Repentance. Jews who are 13 years old and over fast on Yom Kippur. They do not eat or drink anything for a whole day. The day begins just before the sun goes down on Yom Kippur. It ends just after sundown the next day.

On the eve of Yom Kippur, the synagogue service begins with the chanting of a prayer of repentance, Kol Nidre (COLE NID-ruh). Many Jews spend the rest of the evening and most of the next day praying in the synagogue. Yom Kippur ends at sundown with the blowing of the shofar (SHOW-far).

Inside of synagogue

What is a shofar?

A shofar is a musical instrument made from a ram's horn. It sounds something like a trumpet or a few oboes played together. The shofar that Jews used thousands of years ago could be heard for miles. Sometimes it warned people of danger. It also told people when to go to the temple to pray. The modern shofar is smaller and not as loud. Jewish people listen to the sound of the shofar on Rosh Hashanah and Yom Kippur. It reminds them to think seriously about their lives.

Cantor blowing a shofar

On Rosh Hashanah people eat pieces of apple dipped in honey–sweet food to start off a sweet year!

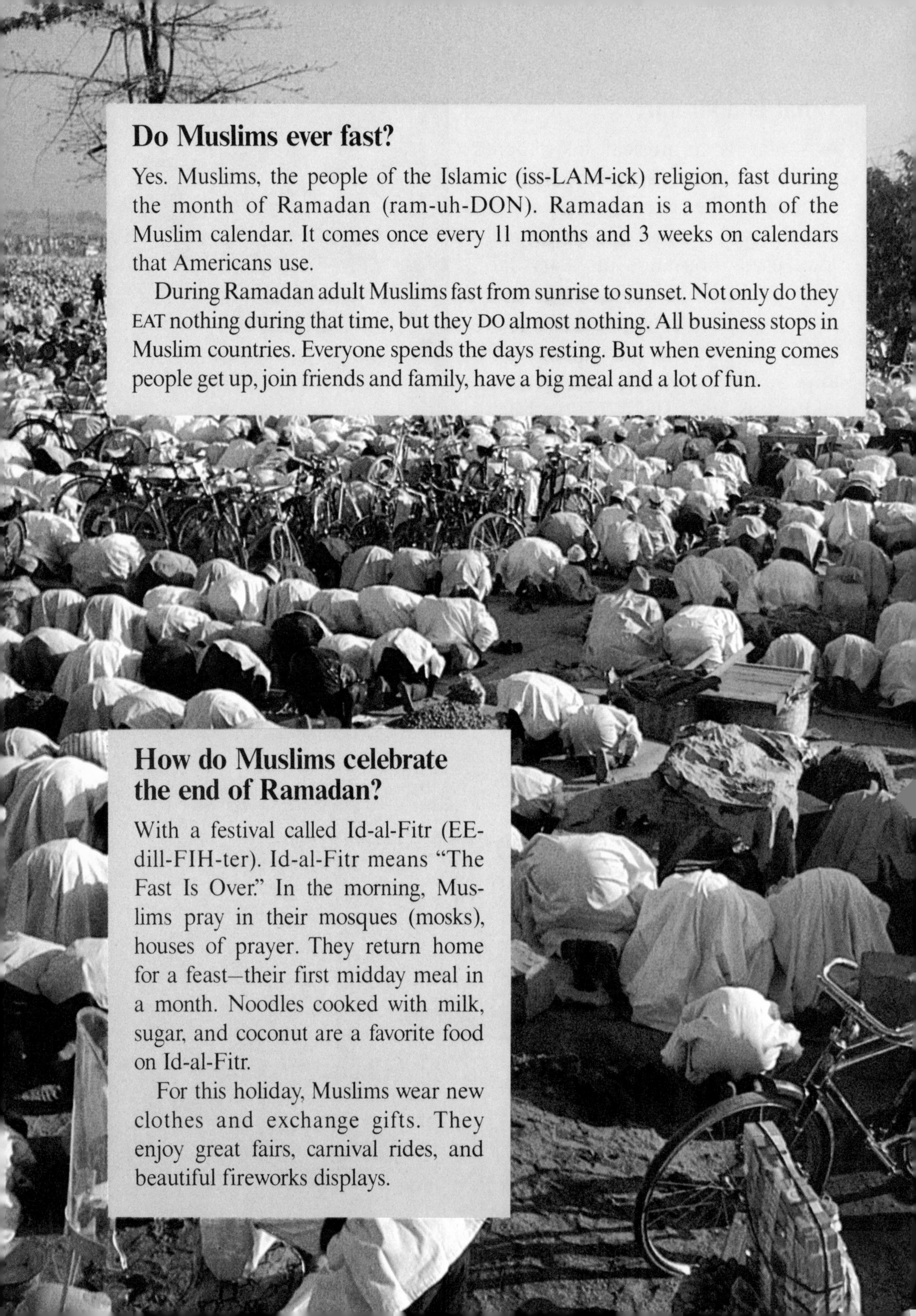

Do Muslims ever fast?

Yes. Muslims, the people of the Islamic (iss-LAM-ick) religion, fast during the month of Ramadan (ram-uh-DON). Ramadan is a month of the Muslim calendar. It comes once every 11 months and 3 weeks on calendars that Americans use.

During Ramadan adult Muslims fast from sunrise to sunset. Not only do they EAT nothing during that time, but they DO almost nothing. All business stops in Muslim countries. Everyone spends the days resting. But when evening comes people get up, join friends and family, have a big meal and a lot of fun.

How do Muslims celebrate the end of Ramadan?

With a festival called Id-al-Fitr (EE-dill-FIH-ter). Id-al-Fitr means "The Fast Is Over." In the morning, Muslims pray in their mosques (mosks), houses of prayer. They return home for a feast–their first midday meal in a month. Noodles cooked with milk, sugar, and coconut are a favorite food on Id-al-Fitr.

For this holiday, Muslims wear new clothes and exchange gifts. They enjoy great fairs, carnival rides, and beautiful fireworks displays.

What happens on Ground Hog Day?

According to an old tradition the ground hog, or woodchuck, wakes up from its winter sleep on February 2. The animal is supposed to come out of its hole and become a weather forecaster. If the ground hog sees its shadow, the story goes, it becomes frightened and goes back into the den for more sleep. This is supposed to mean six more weeks of winter. But if the ground hog doesn't see its shadow, it won't be frightened. It stays up to search for food. This is supposed to mean spring will be coming soon.

Who brought the Ground Hog Day tradition to America?

Both the Germans and the English. For hundreds of years Germans have watched the badger on February 2. They say the badger's behavior on that day will tell them whether spring is coming early or late. The English have watched the hedgehog for the same reason. German and English settlers in America began watching the ground hog to continue the tradition.

Opposite: Nigerian Moslems bowed in prayer

What is Martin Luther King, Jr., Day?

It is a special day to remember Martin Luther King, Jr., a famous black American civil rights leader and minister. He worked peacefully to bring about equal rights for black Americans. Many states honor the memory of Martin Luther King, Jr., on January 15, his birthday.

Do all Americans celebrate Lincoln's Birthday?

No. Only 25 states of the United States celebrate Lincoln's Birthday, February 12, as a separate holiday. Four more states put Lincoln's Birthday and Washington's Birthday together into President's Day. Some Southern states don't celebrate Lincoln's Birthday at all because Lincoln was President during the Civil War. At the start of that war, the South withdrew from the United States. President Lincoln's army fought the Southern army and brought the South back into the country.

When is Susan B. Anthony Day?

On her birthday, February 15. Susan B. Anthony was an American who lived in the 1800s. At that time women were not allowed to vote in elections. Susan B. Anthony fought very hard to get women that right. In 1872, she voted and was arrested for it. When she died in 1906, only four states had given women the right to vote. Today every woman in every state has that right.

When do Americans celebrate George Washington's Birthday?

George Washington was born on February 22. But his birthday is now celebrated on the third Monday in February. In this way people can enjoy a long weekend with the holiday.

George Washington was the first President of the United States. He was also Commander in Chief of the army during the American Revolutionary War. Americans fought that war so that they could rule their own country. George Washington is the only American president so far whose birthday people celebrated while he was still alive.

Who was St. Valentine?

Nobody knows for sure, and there are several saints named Valentine. One St. Valentine was a priest and doctor. He lived in the city of Rome about 300 years after the birth of Jesus. The emperor of Rome refused to allow people to be married in a Christian ceremony. St. Valentine ignored the emperor. He continued to perform marriages in the Christian way. When the Romans found out, they sent St. Valentine to prison and executed him. Later, February 14 became St. Valentine's Day, a day to honor one of the St. Valentines. Still later it became simply Valentine's Day, a day for sweethearts.

When did people begin sending valentines to each other?

People started writing valentine love letters in about 1400. Soon some began to draw pictures on their letters. They added lace to make their valentines prettier. Once people sent valentines only to their sweethearts. But today people send valentines to friends and family, too.

Valentine's Day is very popular in England, France, the United States, and Canada.

Why do Irish people celebrate St. Patrick's Day?

St. Patrick is the patron saint of Ireland. He introduced Christianity to Ireland. St. Patrick's Day is both a holy day and a national holiday in Ireland. It is popular also in American cities in which many Irish families live. A lot of non-Irish people enjoy it, too. St. Patrick's Day is March 17, the anniversary of his death more than 1,500 years ago.

Was St. Patrick Irish?

No! St. Patrick wasn't born in Ireland. He was probably born in Wales. He called himself "Patricus," a Latin name which means "well-born." Patricus is Patrick in English.

St. Patrick went to Ireland as a slave. He had been captured by Irish raiders who knew nothing of Christianity. Later he escaped and returned to his home where he became a Christian bishop. He went back to Ireland to teach Christianity to the people there.

Why do people wear green on St. Patrick's Day?

St. Patrick's Day is an Irish holiday, and green has almost always been connected with Ireland. Perhaps this is because the hills of Ireland look so green. There is a legend that says that in Ireland's landscape there are 40 shades of green. Also, shamrocks, small three-leaved plants, grow wild in Ireland and stay green the year round.

Did St. Patrick drive the snakes out of Ireland?

There are no snakes in Ireland today. A legend says that St. Patrick drove them out by beating on a drum. However, some people believe that Ireland never had any snakes.

Snakes have long been connected with evil and evil doings. St. Patrick was a good man. So some people think the legend means that St. Patrick drove evil out of Ireland.

What is Lent?

Lent is the time each year when Christians prepare themselves for Easter. It is the 40 days (not counting Sundays) from Ash Wednesday to Easter Day. The 40 days remind Christians of the time Jesus spent praying and fasting in the wilderness.

The word "Lent" comes from an old word for spring, "lengthentide," when the days are lengthening (growing longer). Lent begins in February or early March depending on when Easter Sunday itself comes.

A long time ago Christians followed strict rules of fasting during Lent. They did not eat anything with eggs, milk, meat, or animal fat in them. The rules are less strict today. But Christians are still expected to live simply and to ask God's forgiveness for their sins.

Lent is a time when Christians are expected to think about the needs of other people. As a sign of their faith, some people deny themselves (give up) a favorite food or activity for 40 days. Sharing whatever is given up is another chance to help people in need.

Why do some people have ashes on their foreheads on Ash Wednesday?

Christian churches have special Ash Wednesday services at the start of Lent. In some churches, ashes are used to mark small crosses on the foreheads of the people. Ashes are an ancient symbol of sorrow. They remind people to be sorry for their sins during Lent.

The ashes used in churches on Ash Wednesday are made by burning the palm branches used on Palm Sunday the year before. Palm Sunday is the Sunday before Easter.

What do pretzels have to do with Lent?

At one time Christians ate pretzels only during Lent. Pretzels are made from plain dough sprinkled with salt. They have no milk, eggs, or animal fat—foods Christains were not supposed to eat as they prepared for Easter.

"Pretzel" comes from a Latin word for "little arms." The twist in the thin bread looks like arms folded in prayer.

Some people in Europe still never eat pretzels except during Lent.

What do hot cross buns have to do with Lent?

Hot cross buns are sweet cakes decorated with a sugar cross on top. Many Christians eat them during Lent.

Hot cross buns were first baked in Europe. Nobody knows exactly when. One tradition dates the custom from 1361 when a Christian monk baked hot cross buns to give to poor people.

What is Mardi Gras?

Mardi Gras (MAR-dee grah) is a festival day on the Tuesday before the beginning of Lent. The Mardi Gras celebration began in France. It is the day that ends a season of parades, parties, and carnivals.

"Mardi Gras" means "fat Tuesday" in French. It dates from the time when Christians had to use up all animal fat before Lent. From early January until the night before Ash Wednesday, the French people would celebrate. The biggest festival of all was on "fat Tuesday."

Today, Mardi Gras carnivals are popular in many European cities. Rio de Janeiro, Brazil, has a grand carnival, too.

Some Christians call the day before Lent begins Shrove Tuesday. "Shrove" is an old word that means "to confess sins." On Shrove Tuesday people would go to church, confess their sins, and then go home for a big party.

Do any people in the United States celebrate Mardi Gras?

Yes. French settlers brought the Mardi Gras festival to the United States. Cities in Alabama, Florida, Louisiana, Mississippi, and Texas have colorful Mardi Gras celebrations. The biggest is in New Orleans, Louisiana. Many families of French background still live there.

How do people in New Orleans celebrate Mardi Gras?

With a carnival that lasts for ten days. People come from all over the United States to join the fun. They wear masks and fancy costumes, go to parties and balls, and watch parades. Groups called Krewes sponsor the events. Each Krewe names a king and queen for its parade, a custom dating back hundreds of years to carnivals in Europe.

The biggest parade and parties are on the last day of the carnival. A Krewe called the Rex Organization ("Rex" is a Latin word meaning "king") chooses the king of the whole carnival. There is a parade with bands and gigantic floats. Huge torches light the floats. Everyone wears a mask–except the king of the carnival–and dances until dawn.

What is Pancake Day?

People in England celebrate Pancake Day on Shrove Tuesday, the day before Lent begins. Long ago Christians were not supposed to eat fats, milk, and eggs during Lent. So they make pancakes to use up those foods.

Children in England like to play toss-the-pancake on Pancake Day. Someone throws a pancake high in the air. Children jump up and try to grab it. Whoever catches the biggest piece of pancake wins a prize.

What is a Pancake Day Race?

A Pancake Day Race takes place in Olney, England, every year. Women run carrying a frying pan in which a pancake is still cooking. They must flip the pancake three times during the race. Each racer wears a hat, and an apron over her dress. Slacks are not allowed. The winner receives a kiss from the person who rings the bell to start the race. Winner and runner-up each receive a prayer book.

Some people say the custom began in 1445. On the day before Lent began, people were on their way to church. A woman making pancakes heard the church bell ring. She ran to church still wearing an apron and holding the frying pan in her hand.

Do people in the United States celebrate Pancake Day?

Yes. The townspeople of Liberal, Kansas, hold a Pancake Day Race. The winner gets prizes. After the race is over the people of Liberal, Kansas, talk by telephone to the people of Olney, England.

What is Holy Week for Christians?

Holy Week is the week before Easter. It begins on Palm Sunday, another joyful day for Christians. On Palm Sunday, many churchgoers receive branches or leaves of palm trees. The palms remind Christians of Christ's triumphal entry into the city of Jerusalem. There, a few days before his death, he was hailed as a king. The joyous crowd who greeted him strewed his path with palms.

Monday, Tuesday, and Wednesday of Holy Week have no special names. Thursday is called Maundy (or Holy) Thursday. "Maundy" comes from a Latin word used in a hymn often sung on the Thursday of Holy Week. Maundy Thursday keeps the memory of the Last Supper when Jesus introduced Holy Communion. Jesus and his disciples (dih-SIE-pulls)–his closest followers–were all Jews and celebrated Passover. The Last Supper was a Passover meal that Jesus ate with his disciples.

Good Friday is the saddest day of the year for Christians. On Good Friday, Christians remember the crucifixion and burial of Jesus. Such a sad day is called "good" because of all the good that Jesus brought into the world. The Greeks call the day "Great Friday."

The day before Easter is Holy (or Low) Saturday. Churches have no services that day. Some drape their doors in black cloth. The black represents the time Jesus spent in his tomb.

Portrait of Christ by Rembrandt

Why do Christians celebrate Easter?

Easter is the happiest and most important Christian holy day. On Easter Christians celebrate their belief in the resurrection (rez-uh-RECK-shun) of Jesus Christ on the third day after his crucifixion (crew-suh-FIK-shun). "Resurrection" means "a rising from the dead." "Crucifixion" means "being put to death on a cross."

The Christian religion teaches that Jesus's resurrection is a great victory over death. It brings new and everlasting life to all who believe in Jesus.

The English word "Easter" probably comes from "Eostre," the name of an old goddess whose festival was in the spring. Easter is always in the spring.

Easter celebration at St. Patrick's Cathedral, New York City

Why does the date of Easter change from year to year?

Because Easter was first celebrated according to the ancient Jewish calendar—not the Roman calendar used today. Easter is always on Sunday. But it can come as early as March 22 or as late as April 25.

For a long time, Christians observed Easter at the same time that Jews celebrated Passover. Passover can begin on Sunday, Tuesday, Thursday, or Saturday. The Christians wanted Easter on Sunday since they believe Jesus rose from the dead on the first day of the week. The Christians were also slowly giving up the use of the Jewish calendar in favor of the Roman one. So in the year 325, the Christians made a change. They decided on a formula for setting the date of Easter. Easter is the first Sunday following the first full moon in the spring.

Why is the egg an Easter symbol?

In many of the world's cultures the egg stands for new life. An egg looks like a stone or a rock. But it is from an egg that new life bursts forth. The egg is a reminder to Christians of the resurrection of Jesus.

When did people begin to decorate eggs at Easter?

No one is certain. Some people think the Egyptians colored eggs in the spring long before Jesus was born. Before dye was invented, people colored eggs by wrapping them in leaves and flowers and dropping them in boiling water. This gave the eggs the color of green leaves or red petals. Later, Christians painted eggs and had them blessed. They ate some and gave the others to friends as Easter gifts.

How do people in Europe decorate Easter eggs?

Germans decorate empty eggshells. First they make a tiny hole in each end of a raw egg. Next they blow the egg out of its shell. Then they color the outside of the unbroken eggshell. Greek Christians exchange bright-red eggs. The people who live in the Ukraine (you-CRANE), a part of the Soviet Union, decorate Easter eggs with pictures. Some are of fir trees, bell towers, or chapels.

Why does the Easter bunny carry colored eggs?

In many cultures, the white hare–like the egg–stands for new life. There are many old stories about hares and eggs.

A German legend says that a poor woman once hid colored eggs in a nest. They were to be an Easter gift for her children. Just as the children saw the nest, a hare hopped away. So people said the hare brought the eggs.

Today people call the Easter hare the Easter bunny.

What happens on the day after Easter in Washington, D.C.?

Children roll Easter eggs on the White House lawn. Dolly Madison began the custom when her husband, James, was president (1808–1816).

Children try to roll their hard-boiled eggs as far as possible without breaking them. There are no other rules for egg rolling. As many as 50,000 people watch or take part in the event. Many hope to get a look at the president, who comes out to watch.

Easter-egg-rolling contest at the White House

What is an Easter parade?

It's a parade of people, all dressed up for Easter. Many people wear new clothes on Easter. After church some of them go for a walk. Europeans used to say prayers and sing religous songs on Easter walks. Today people call an Easter walk an Easter parade. There is no music at an Easter parade. People just walk up and down the street. In years when hats are in style, women show off their fancy Easter bonnets. Sometimes famous people join the Easter parade on Fifth Avenue in New York City.

What is Passover?

Passover is a happy Jewish holiday. It celebrates the Jews' escape from slavery in Egypt more than 3,000 years ago. For most Jews the holiday lasts eight days. During that time they eat special foods, such as matzos (MOTT-suhz), that remind them of their ancestors' escape. Jewish families invite their relatives and friends to join them on the eve of the first two days for a seder (SAY-dur), a special meal and religious service.

What happens at a seder?

During a seder, Jewish people sit around the dining table and read aloud from a book called the Haggadah (huh-GAH-duh). It tells the story of the Jews' slavery and escape to freedom. "Haggadah" means "story" in Hebrew. On the table are a plate of matzos and a plate of special foods: horseradish; parsley or celery; a mixture of wine with crushed apples, almonds, and cinnamon; a lamb's shankbone; and a roasted egg. They are symbols of Jewish slavery and deliverance. The seder also includes prayers, songs, and a big Passover meal.

What do the special foods on a Passover table stand for?

Each of the special foods on the seder plate stands for something else. The horseradish, called maror (mah-RORE) in Hebrew, is a bitter herb. It reminds Jews of the bitterness of slavery in Egypt. It also recalls the bitter fate of those modern Jews who live in countries that don't allow them to follow the laws of their faith.

The parsley or celery, called carpas (CAR-pahss), is a reminder of the poor food supply the ancient Jewish slaves lived on. During the seder ceremony, a piece of carpas is dipped into salt water. The salt water stands for the tears of the slaves.

The wine-apple-almond-cinnamon mixture is called haroset (har-O-set). It represents the mortar, or cement, that the Jewish slaves had to mix as they worked for their Egyptian masters.

The shankbone stands for the lamb that was offered by Jews as a sacrifice to God in ancient days. The roasted egg, still in its shell, is a symbol of a special sacrifice offered during early Passover celebrations. The egg is called baitza (bait-ZAH).

Why do Jewish people eat matzos on Passover?

Eating matzos reminds Jews of their escape from slavery in Egypt. During that escape, the Jews had no time to bake bread. Bread needs time to rise, or puff up, before it is baked. So the Jews baked flat breads, without yeast. They were something like matzos, which are also made without yeast.

Dinner table set for Passover seder

What is Arbor Day?

Arbor Day is a special day for planting trees. There is no set date for Arbor Day in the United States. But many states celebrate Arbor Day in May. The first Arbor Day celebration in the United States took place in Nebraska on April 10, 1872. On that day people in Nebraska planted a million trees. Some holidays celebrate the past, but Arbor Day is dedicated to the future. Trees prevent floods and keep the topsoil from blowing away. A tree is the symbol of life in many cultures.

How did April Fools' Day get started?

No one is sure how April Fools' Day got started. Most countries seem to have a day when people play tricks on each other. Children especially like these days.

Some people think that trick days began in India. People there celebrate a spring holiday called Holi (HOE-lee). A favorite trick on Holi is to fill a bamboo pipe with colored powder and blow the powder at people. Sometimes children fill the pipe with water and squirt each other.

How do people in Japan celebrate Buddha's Birthday?

People in Japan celebrate Buddha's (BOO-duz) Birthday with a flower festival on April 8.

Buddha was a great religious leader in India. He lived about 500 years before Jesus was born. He taught people to stay calm and to be kind to one another. In that way, he said, they could find peace and happiness. His followers spread his teachings throughout Asia.

On Buddha's Birthday millions of Japanese Buddhists go to their neighborhood temples carrying fresh flowers. There they wash a small statue of Buddha with sweet tea. Little girls cover their faces with white powder so they will look clean and fresh for Buddha. Children wear silk kimonos (robes) that are decorated with fresh flowers. Buddhist priests march through the streets wearing costumes of olden days. Many floats pass by in a parade. One float always carries a statue of Buddha on a huge white elephant. In India only important royalty were allowed to ride on white elephants. The statue of Buddha on an elephant shows how important he is to the Buddhists.

What is May Day?

It is an ancient holiday in which people dance around a large pole with streamers hanging down. The pole is called a Maypole. May Day is celebrated on May 1 in many countries of Europe.

When did Americans start celebrating Mother's Day?

The first Mother's Day celebration in the United States took place in 1873 in Boston. But it was not until 1915 that Mother's Day became a national holiday. Ever since then Americans honor their mothers on the second Sunday in May.

When did Americans begin to celebrate Father's Day?

People in Spokane, Washington, celebrated the first Father's Day in 1910. Mrs. John Brice Dodd, who lived in Spokane, thought that fathers should be honored with a special day. She talked to her minister about it. He, a few other ministers, and the YMCA convinced people to celebrate Father's Day. The idea spread to other cities and states. In 1924 President Coolidge asked people all over the United States to honor their fathers with a special day. Ever since then, Americans celebrate Father's Day on the third Sunday in June.

Why do Canadians celebrate Victoria Day?

Canada is part of the British Commonwealth—a group of countries that either are or once were under English rule. Victoria Day celebrates the birthday of Queen Victoria. She ruled England and the Commonwealth for 64 years (1837–1901). After she died, people continued to celebrate her birthday, May 24. Modern Canadians celebrate the holiday on the Monday that comes just before May 25. In this way, Canadians have a long holiday weekend.

Is there a Children's Day?

Yes. Many Protestant churches in the United States celebrate Children's Day. It is the second Sunday in June. Children who belong to the church take part in religious programs—songs, stories, and plays. On that day, the children are sometimes promoted from one Sunday school class to the next.

Throughout history other countries have celebrated special children's days in various ways. One unusual custom is practiced in Yugoslavia. Parents tie up their children on that country's Children's Day. They set the children free when they promise to be good for the rest of the year.

How do Americans honor the men and women who served in wars?

The United States has two holidays to honor people who were part of the armed services. Veterans Day, November 11, honors all men and women who served in the army, navy, marine corps, and coast guard. Memorial Day honors American soldiers who died in wars. Memorial Day used to be called Decoration Day because people decorated the graves of soldiers with flowers. It is celebrated on the last Monday in May.

Most Southern states have their own Memorial Day. Many celebrate it in April or May. On this holiday Southerners remember soldiers who fought in the Civil War—a war in which the Southern states fought the Northern states. On Memorial Day, they decorate the graves of soldiers who fought for the South.

Canadians have a holiday a lot like Memorial Day. It is called Remembrance Day. This holiday is celebrated on the same day as Veterans Day in the United States. It is the day World War I ended.

Marine Corps War Memorial, Arlington, Virginia

How do French Canadians celebrate Jean Baptiste Day?

People who live in Quebec celebrate Jean Baptiste (ZHON-bah-TEEST) Day on June 24 with a parade. Quebec is the French-speaking area of Canada. A favorite float in the parade shows a little boy dressed as a shepherd. He is Jean Baptiste, St. John the Baptist, the patron saint of Quebec. A lamb with a ribbon and bow around its neck stands next to St. John. The lamb stands for Jesus. Great crowds gather in the city of Montreal and cheer little St. John and his lamb.

The Jean Baptiste holiday begins on June 24 and lasts eight days. During that time French-Canadians in Quebec honor the French language and culture.

Why do people in the United States celebrate the Fourth of July?

The Fourth of July is the birthday of the United States of America. In the 1700s, England ruled over 13 colonies along the east coast of what's now the United States. The colonists thought that the English king treated them unfairly. They wanted to rule themselves. In 1776 a group of leaders from the colonies met in Philadelphia. They talked about independence from England. Thomas Jefferson wrote down their thoughts in the paper called the Declaration of Independence. It said that the colonists wanted to be free, and it told why. The Fourth of July was the day the Declaration of Independence was finished. Four days later it was read to a large crowd of people. Bells rang and the people cheered. A new country was born. But it had to fight and win a war with England before it became a free country–the United States of America.

Bastille Day parade, Paris

Why do the French celebrate Bastille Day?

The Bastille (ba-STEEL) was a French prison. The French king sent many people there who displeased him. On July 14, 1789, French rebels attacked the prison and freed the prisoners. They destroyed the Bastille. The capture of the Bastille by the rebels stands for freedom to the French people. Bastille Day is a great national holiday in France. The French celebrate it with music, parades, and dancing in the streets.

When do Americans celebrate Flag Day?

People in the United States celebrate Flag Day on June 14. On that day in 1777, leaders of the American colonies voted to accept a new flag as the symbol of their country. Before that they flew the Grand Union flag. It had a small design of the English flag on it. The new flag had 13 stars on it instead—to stand for the 13 colonies.

There is a legend of how a seamstress named Betsy Ross made the first American flag. The story goes that General George Washington wanted the stars to have six points. But Betsy talked him into using five-pointed stars instead.

When do Canadians celebrate Dominion Day?

Canadians celebrate Dominion Day on July 1. Dominion Day is Canada's birthday. Like the United States, Canada was once ruled by England. On July 1, 1867, the English decided to make Canada into a dominion. A dominion makes its own laws. But it is still loyal to another country (like England) that has a king or queen. Some Canadians call Dominion Day "Canada Day." On that day Canadians display flags and watch parades. The Canadian mounted police wear their bright red jackets.

Celebration in Ottawa, Canada

What is Labor Day?

The United States and Canada have their own day to honor workers. It is called Labor Day. The word "labor" means "work." Labor Day is celebrated in both countries on the first Monday in September.

Is there a holiday for pets?

Yes. In the United States, there is a National Pet Health Week in October. During that week people are reminded to have their pets checked by an animal doctor every year. In September there is a Pet Responsibility Week. The purpose of that week is to remind people to learn how to take good care of their pets.

Why do people in North and South America celebrate Columbus Day?

To honor Christopher Columbus, who landed in America on October 12, 1492. Many people say that Columbus was not the first European to discover America. The Irish and Norwegians claim their explorers came to America first. But no one paid much attention to their discoveries. Columbus's discovery caused Europeans to realize that a new land—America—existed.

Columbus didn't know that he discovered America. He thought he'd landed near China or Japan!

Why do people celebrate Halloween?

Halloween is a combination of holidays. As a night of ghosts and witches it was started by the Celts (selts). They were people who lived in France and the British Isles hundreds of years ago.

The Celts had a holiday called Samhain (SAH-win), which meant "end of summer." So Samhain was a festival marking the end of the food-growing season. The Celts believed that spirits of the fruits and vegetables, and also the ghosts of people, visited the earth on Samhain, which was October 31. The Celts lit huge bonfires on hilltops to scare the ghosts away.

Years later, the Celts became Christians. They and other Christians celebrated Allhallows Day (now called All Saints' Day) on November 1. It was a day to remember important Christians who had died. The Celts called the night before (October 31) Allhallows E'en, or holy evening. "Allhallows E'en" was later shortened to "Halloween."

Many of the customs of Samhain were continued on Halloween. Almost all spooky Halloween practices were started by the Celts.

Why did people believe that witches traveled on broomsticks on Halloween?

In Europe a few hundred years ago, there were people who called themselves witches. They worshiped the devil the way most people worship a god. They claimed they could perform witchcraft, or magic. The witches held large meetings called Sabbats. There they gathered around a big fire where they cooked up magical potions. Some of these were drugs the witches drank. Sometimes the drugs caused them to imagine themselves flying through the air. There were always brooms near the fire to sweep it clean. So stories got started that witches used magic to fly about on broomsticks.

The Sabbat held on Allhallows E'en was a special one. People believed that the witches flew to this Sabbat on broomsticks.

How did trick or treat get started?

Trick or treat began in Ireland. People went from house to house and begged for food on Halloween. They promised good luck to those who gave and bad luck to those who didn't.

Who was Jack-o'-Lantern?

To the Celts, Jack-o'-Lantern was the spirit of the pumpkin. The Celts carved a pleasant-looking pumpkin face to show Jack as a good spirit, not a nasty one.

The Irish claim that Jack-o-Lantern was a person who couldn't get into heaven because he was too stingy. But the devil didn't want him, either. So ever since, he's had to wander about carrying a lantern. The Irish had no pumpkins, so they used to make Jack-o'-Lanterns from turnips and potatoes.

Why do people wear spooky costumes on Halloween?

The custom of wearing spooky costumes on Halloween began with a group of Irish Celts called Druids. The Irish believed that evil spirits roamed about the earth on Halloween. The Druids wanted to fool the evil spirits into thinking that they were spirits, too. So they dressed as ghosts and goblins.

Is there really a Great Pumpkin?

Not even Linus can answer that question. And he's been waiting for the Great Pumpkin to show up for years!

Jack-o'-lantern

Why do people in England celebrate Guy Fawkes Day?

Guy Fawkes Day, November 5, celebrates the capture of an English traitor named Guy Fawkes. In 1605, he and some friends planned to blow up the Houses of Parliament with the king inside. (Parliament is something like the Congress of the United States.) Someone wrote a letter to a member of Parliament. It warned him of the plot. Searchers discovered 36 barrels of gunpowder in the cellar. They arrested Guy Fawkes just as he was about to light the gunpowder. He and his helpers were executed.

The Clock Tower of the Houses of Parliament

How do the English celebrate Guy Fawkes Day?

With mischief making! At night people march in noisy parades. Children ring bells, crash cymbals, and bang pots. They make a great deal of noise. People stuff a dummy of Guy Fawkes with straw and burn it on top of a large bonfire. They light firecrackers. They sing and yell while Guy Fawkes burns.

When is Election Day?

The Tuesday after the first Monday in November is Election Day in the United States. Election Day is a legal holiday in most states. That means people get the day off from work and school. Every four years United States citizens vote for a new president and vice-president. During other years, they vote for state governors, city mayors, or judges. Sometimes they vote for members of Congress.

In Canada and England there is no regular national election day. National elections in Canada and England can be called at any time.

Why do we eat turkey on Thanksgiving Day?

Eating turkey on Thanksgiving is a tradition that started when the Pilgrims ate turkey on the first Thanksgiving. The Pilgrims were a group of English people who came to America in 1620. During their first winter in their new land, they didn't have enough food. Many died. But that spring, their Indian neighbors taught them to plant corn. The Indians showed the Pilgrims where to catch fish. They taught the Pilgrims how to use fish to make the soil richer. By fall, it was clear there would be plenty of food for the next winter.

Because they were thankful, the Pilgrims decided to have a feast—the first Thanksgiving celebration. This took place in 1621. And what better way to celebrate than with plenty of food! The Indians were invited to the feast, of course.

For the occasion, the Pilgrim men hunted deer and turkeys. Turkeys ran wild during those days. Somehow, the tradition lasted, and we eat turkey every year on Thanksgiving Day.

Benjamin Franklin loved turkeys. He wanted the turkey to be the national bird of the United States.

Do Canadians celebrate Thanksgiving?

Yes, on the second Monday in October. Canadians claim that the first Thanksgiving ever celebrated in North America took place in Canada in 1578. In both Canada and the United States, people celebrate Thanksgiving in much the same way. Turkey is a favorite food in both countries.

Menorah

Why do Jewish people celebrate Hanukkah?

Hanukkah, or Chanukkah, (HAH-nuh-kuh), celebrates a victory and the rededication of the Jewish temple more than 2,500 years ago. In the second century before Jesus was born, a Greek ruler in Syria had taken over the Jewish land where Israel is now. He had also taken over the Jews' temple in Jerusalem. For three years the Jews fought until they won back their temple and some of their land. They rededicated the temple to God.

The Jews wanted to relight their temple lamps, which the invaders had let go out. But there was only enough holy oil for one day. A legend says a miracle happened. The lamps were lit and that tiny bit of oil burned for eight days. By then, more holy oil had been made. Because of this, Hanukkah is also called the Festival of Lights.

Hanukkah comes during the month of December. People celebrate it for eight days in memory of the eight days that the oil burned.

How do Jewish people celebrate Hanukkah?

Every night of Hanukkah, Jews light candles and recite special festival blessings. The Hanukkah candle holder is called a menorah (muh-NOR-uh). A menorah has space for nine candles—one for each night of Hanukkah plus a shammash (shah-MASH), or a serving candle. On the first night, one candle and the shammash are lighted. Each night one more candle is lighted. On the last night, all the candles are burning.

During Hanukkah, Jews eat special holiday foods, usually cooked in oil. Many eat potato pancakes called latkes (LAHT-kuz). They sing songs and exchange gifts. Children receive Hanukkah gelt—money. Sometimes they also get pieces of chocolate wrapped in gold foil that look like gold coins. And they have fun playing with a top called a dreidel (DRAY-dill).

Dreidel

When did people begin to celebrate Christmas?

No one knows the day and month of Jesus's birth. It was a long time before Christians had a set date for celebrating Christmas. About the year 350, a church in Rome decided Christ's Mass, a church service marking the birth of Jesus, should be on December 25. This became popular. People called Christ's Mass "Christmas."

The Christmas tree at The Metropolitan Museum of Art

Who decorated the first Christmas tree?

No one knows for sure. The custom of bringing an evergreen tree indoors and decorating it at Christmas started in Germany. One legend says that Martin Luther started the practice. Luther was an important Christian leader. According to the story, he noticed the starlit sky as he walked home one Christmas Eve about the year 1513. He thought the stars looked as if they were shining on the branches. When he arrived home, Martin Luther placed a small fir tree inside his house. He decorated it with lighted candles.

Decorating Christmas trees became popular in Germany. Prince Albert, the German husband of Queen Victoria, took the tradition to England. Both German and English people brought it to America.

Did people always sing Christmas carols?

Christmas has had its own music and songs since it started. But Christmas carols have a special history. The word "carol" means "circle dance." Among many ancient people, caroling was common at festivals. Groups would dance arm-in-arm, often singing simple, happy songs. Carols became a natural way for Christians to express their joy at Christmas.

Christmas carols were known in England by the year 1100. St. Francis of Assisi (uh-SEE-zee), who lived in Italy about 800 years ago, encouraged the singing of Christmas carols. He is sometimes called the Father of the Christmas Carol.

What special game do Mexican children play at Christmas?

They like to break the piñata (peen-YAH-tuh). A piñata is a clay pot that Mexicans make in many shapes. Sometimes a piñata looks like a fat person, a clown, an animal, or Santa Claus. It is filled with Christmas treats such as candy, nuts, and small gifts.

Someone hangs the piñata from the ceiling or a doorway. It is just above the children's reach. A leader blindfolds them one at a time and leads them to the piñata. Everyone hopes to get a turn. The leader gives the blindfolded child a stick. The child takes three swings at the piñata while the other children circle around it. They dance and sing.

When the piñata breaks, everyone scrambles for the Christmas treats.

Who was the first Santa Claus?

Many people say that Nicholas, the bishop of Myra, was the first Santa Claus. Nicholas lived in what is now part of Turkey about 300 years after Jesus was born. Very little is known about him. But he is supposed to have loved children and to have given them presents.

Nicholas became a popular saint in Europe. He is the patron saint of Russia. His special day is December 6. "Santa Claus" is the English for "Sinter Claes," the Dutch name for St. Nicholas.

Did people always believe that reindeer pulled Santa's sleigh?

No. Through the years people have believed many different things about how Santa Claus traveled. Some people believed that Santa traveled on a donkey or a horse. Others believed that he traveled across the sky in a chariot pulled by horses. But people who lived in Scandinavian countries were always certain that Santa traveled in a sleigh pulled by reindeer. How else could he travel through icy Northern Europe?

What is a Yule log?

A Yule log is a big log of wood that some people burn on Christmas Eve. Before the time of Jesus, Scandinavians had a holiday called Yule. They celebrated Yule at about the time of year that people today celebrate Christmas. On Yule they lighted huge logs. The fires were supposed to make the sun shine brighter. After Scandinavians became Christians, they continued to burn Yule logs. The custom of burning Yule logs at Christmas spread throughout Europe, including England.

What's the best holiday of the year?

Everybody has his or her own favorite holiday. Snoopy likes Easter because he gets to play the role of the Easter Beagle. Lucy likes April Fools' Day. She enjoys fooling Charlie Brown. Charlie Brown doesn't like any holidays. They remind him of the cards he never gets!

Did You Know That...

Kamehameha (kah-MAY-hah-MAY-hah) Day in Hawaii is the only holiday in the United States that honors royalty. King Kamehameha I lived from 1758 to 1819. He united all the islands of Hawaii into one kingdom. On June 11, Hawaiians hold pageants, parades, and feasts in King Kamehameha's honor. Enormous flower garlands called leis (layz) are placed on the king's statue in Honolulu.

Statue of King Kamehameha

Many official holidays are the birthdays of famous men and women. But your own birthday is important, too! In many places it's a tradition to have a birthday cake with a candle for each year on it. It's good luck to blow out all the candles with one breath. In some countries, children are often named after saints. Each saint has a special feast day, and people celebrate on their saint's day. If your name is Ann, you celebrate on July 26; Saint Jerome's day is September 30. Sometimes people celebrate their saint's day and their own birthday, too!

People in Mexico celebrate the Days of the Dead on the first and second of November. On those days the spirits of the dead are welcomed back to earth for a "visit." Mexicans are very busy before this holiday. They buy new dishes, candlesticks, skeleton dolls, special breads, and candy made in spooky shapes. On October 31 everybody stays up all night decorating altars with flowers and candles. Cookies, candy, and toys are left on the altar for the souls of children. A special meal is prepared in the honor of all the returning souls. Neighbors visit each other and talk about the people they are honoring.

Boxing Day is a British holiday that has nothing to do with people punching one another. Many years ago in England, people gave presents or "boxes" to their servants on the day after Christmas. Today on Boxing Day people give gifts to the postman and other workers.

VOLUME 12 WAS REALLY FUN. WASN'T IT, WOODSTOCK?

YOU'RE RIGHT. WE LEARNED A LOT, TOO!

YOU KNOW, I MAY HAVE BEEN WRONG ABOUT THOSE CHRISTMAS STOCKINGS...

IF YOU WANT TO HANG UP A CHRISTMAS STOCKING, LITTLE FRIEND, I THINK YOU SHOULD!

HANG UP AS MANY AS YOU WANT! MERRY CHRISTMAS!!

SCHULZ